The **John King** was launched at the Charles Hill shipyard in Bristol on 21 October 1935 and delivered to C J King and Sons in February 1936. Her final task for the King company was to escort the **Great Britain** in the River Avon after the latter's return to Bristol on 6 July 1970. This event will be covered in Volume 2. The tug was then purchased by local operator F A Ashmead & Son and renamed **Peter Leigh**. Her main task was to tow African hardwood logs in barges from Avonmouth across the River Severn to Lydney for manufacture into plywood and veneers. The trade is exemplified in the view, dated September 1975, of the tug and barges carrying logs that have been discharged from the Nigerian vessel **River Ethiope**.

(Stuart Kirkby, Bernard McCall collection)

In 1978 the **Peter Leigh** was sold to Bristol Commercial Ships and was renamed **Pride**. It was this company's initials that she carried on her funnel when photographed at Bristol on 2 February 1982. She now saw service well beyond the Bristol Channel. Incidentally, she had been re-engined in 1962, her 4-cylinder Petter of 300bhp being replaced by a 6-cylinder Lister-Blackstone of 337bhp. She was photographed at Bristol on 2 February 1982.

(Danny Lynch)

The *Pride* was sold and renamed **Durdham** in 1986. She was photographed at Avonmouth on 15 February 1988. On 31 October 1988, the **Durdham** broke down off the coast of Devon and had to anchor off Start Point. At the time she was towing an empty barge to Bristol. To get assistance, the tug's skipper boarded a passing yacht but bad weather later in the day meant that the local lifeboat had to take off the remaining crew. The continuing bad weather caused the towline to part and the barge was driven ashore and destroyed. The Salcombe lifeboat and a local diving boat eventually took the **Durdham** into Salcombe harbour. She was repaired and returned to the Bristol Channel.

(Peter Hobday)

We next see her in the City Docks in June 1990. Her hull now seems to be in poor cosmetic condition and her upperworks have evidently been painted in different colours from those seen in the earlier photograph. She was purchased by the Bristol Industrial Museum in 1995 and thankfully has been refurbished to her original fine appearance as we see on the front cover of this book. Also her original name has been restored.

(Bernard McCall)

The **Sea Alarm** was one of a series of tugs built by J Crown & Son at Sunderland. She was constructed as **Empire Ash** for the Ministry of War Transport in 1941. On 15 May 1946, she was sold to Clyde Shipping and renamed **Flying Fulmar**. Purchased by C J King & Sons in May 1956, she remained in service until 1973. Rescued from shipbreakers at Briton Ferry, the **Sea Alarm** was bought by the Welsh Industrial and Maritime Museum and placed in an improvised dry berth constructed from an old lock entrance. The area around was redeveloped in the late 1980s and the tug was totally neglected. She was eventually scrapped during summer 1998. It is thought that her triple expansion steam engine was retained and is stored in Nant Garw. We see her assisting the **Offin River** into Avonmouth in February 1974.

(Bernard McCall collection)

The second vessel of this name, the *Sea Queen* was launched at the Hessle yard of Henry Scarr Ltd on 30 December 1943. She was delivered to the Ministry of War Transport as *Empire Walter* on 20 March 1944 and was one of the 19-strong Birch sub-class. She was managed by the Alexandra Towing Company during her war service. One of her early tasks was to tow parts of the Arromanches harbour across the English Channel after the Normandy invasion. She was acquired by C J King in 1946. In 1953 Her Majesty The Queen and the Duke of Edinburgh opened Bristol's new Council House on College Green. The royal barge landed the royal party in St Augustine's Reach and the immaculate *Sea Queen* was berthed opposite the Queen's landing place. The tug was withdrawn from service in 1973 and laid up at Avonmouth. She eventually left Falmouth in tow of a Spanish tug on 23 June 1974 and arrived at San Esteban de Pravia in Spain three days later. Breaking up began in early September 1974. She was photographed approaching the lock at Avonmouth on 11 July 1970.

(Bernard McCall collection)

5

The **Hermes** was owned in Germany by Bugsier and classified as a salvage tug. In this role she was often based at Dover awaiting an incident in the English Channel. Launched at the Bremerhaven yard of F Schichau in April 1955, she was delivered to Bugsier on 23 July 1956. She was laid up in Bremerhaven in April 1975. After purchase by King in March 1976 to expand the company's deep-sea towage work which had been very successful in 1975, she was renamed **Sea Queen**. Power came from a 6-cylinder Deutz engine of 1420bhp and she was credited with a bollard pull of 18 tonnes. One of her most interesting tasks came in spring 1978. The supertanker **Amoco Cadiz** grounded on the coast of Brittany after a steering failure and with a cargo of 227,000 tonnes of crude oil. The **Sea Queen** was fitted with detergent spraying equipment and was despatched to assist with the clean-up operation. She was photographed at Avonmouth on 19 May 1979. She left the King fleet in the following year and was renamed **Bateleur**. Her end came on 7 August 1983 when she sank off the Ile Sainte Marie near Madagascar.

(Terry Nelder)

Previously named **Foreman**, the **Sea Bristolian** was bought from United Towing, a well-known Humber-based towage company, in October 1972. In the mid-1970s, C J King & Sons widened activities and began to undertake deep-sea towage. The first long tow of the **Sea Bristolian**, for example, saw her delivering trawlers and barges from Pembroke Dock to the Cape Verde Islands and she towed the damaged tanker **Esso Preston** from Cardiff to Aviles in Spain for demolition in March 1975. On the return voyage, she collected a Portuguese minesweeper for delivery to Cairnryan near Stranraer for breaking up. Later in that year she towed the Isle of Man Steam Packet company's vessel **King Orry** from Liverpool to Glasson Dock for breaking. An able seaman sadly lost his life during this tow when he was struck by a towline which suddenly tautened. There is more information about this tug on page 11.

(Peter Hobday)

Built by Henry Scarr at Hessle and costing almost £80,000, the **Sea Alert** was delivered to C J King in April 1960. Her main engine was a 7-cylinder Ruston & Hornsby of 680bhp. In 1993 she was sold to Celtic Diving & Salvage, of Cork, and was renamed **Alert**. In May 1995, she was bought by Labrador Marine Services, of Goose Bay, Labrador, Canada. She underwent various modifications and additions to meet Canadian standards and was used mainly for towing barges and icebergs and for seismic operations. She was wrecked after striking a rock near Nain, Labrador, on 1 November 1995. We see her leaving Avonmouth on 1 May 1971.

(Bernard McCall collection)

The **Sea Volunteer** was launched at the Northwich yard of W J Yarwood & Sons Ltd on 1 December 1962 and completed on 26 March 1963. She was powered by a 7-cylinder Ruston & Hornsby engine of 920bhp. She was one of three King vessels sold after the merger with Cory, details of which are on page 13. Sold in 1983 to Atlantic Tugs and Shipping Ltd, she was refitted and renamed **Wrestler** under the Panamanian flag. In 1987 she was sold via Pounds Marine to undisclosed buyers and converted to a fishing vessel. She was renamed **Immanuel** under the Maltese flag. On 30 July 1987, she foundered in heavy weather when 330 miles south of the Canary Islands.

(Bernard McCall collection)

The **Sea Merrimac** assists T & J Harrison's **Inventor** towards the lock at Avonmouth. The tug was built locally at the Charles Hill shipyard in Bristol. She was launched on 16 June 1964 and handed over to C J King on 4 September. In 1983 she was sold along with the **Sea Volunteer** to Harry Pounds who sold her on to Atlantic Tugs & Shipping Ltd. She was renamed **Pullman** under the Panamanian flag. Two years later, her owners ceased trading after another of its vessels had been involved in smuggling arms. It is assumed that the tug was sold and the next report of her came in 1991 when she was noted at Lanzarote. Sold to Spanish operators in 1992, she was renamed **Cantug** but little is known of her subsequent history.

(Stuart Kirkby, Bernard McCall collection)

The **Sea Bristolian** had been launched at the Beverley shipyard of Cook, Welton & Gemmell on 30 December 1958 and was delivered to United Towing as **Foreman** on 8 May 1959. She was notable in being that company's first seagoing motor tug. Fitted with a Ruston & Hornsby 8-cylinder engine of 1030bhp, she had the appearance of a steam tug with dummy funnel and engine exhaust led up main mast.

We see her assisting the Liberian tanker **Dona Marika** out of the lock and into the choppy Bristol Channel on 2 April 1973. In 1981 she was bought by Mustafa & Najibi & Co for use in the Persian Gulf and was renamed **Mansco Tug 4**. She had been modernised in 1972. She was wrecked on 2 October 1981 off N Pontevedra Bay in north-west Spain.

(Bernard McCall collection)

The **Sea Challenge** was built at the Hessle yard of Richard Dunston. Launched on 4 October 1967, she was completed on 22 December. She was driven by a 6-cylinder Ruston engine of 1350bhp. During the 1970s she was fitted with a Kort nozzle and this improved her bollard pull from 18 tonnes to 22 tonnes. Here we see her on the grid iron located just outside the locks on 9 December 1976. This grid iron, built in 1884/85, is now submerged beneath a huge mass of mud.

(Cedric Catt)

In October 1975 the *Sea Challenge* was sent to collect the Norwegian sail training vessel Christian Radich which had caught fire 200 miles south west of the Scillies. She brought her back to Plymouth and then took her to the Norwegian vessel's home port of Trondheim.

By the early 1980s, it was clear that there was insufficient towage work for the fleets of C J King and Cory and in 1983 the companies merged to form Cory King Towage. All but two of the King vessels were sold. The two retained were the *Sea Challenge* and *Sea Endeavour*. We see the latter on the pages that follow and we then start to look at tugs that have served Cory and the companies into which Cory was eventually subsumed. We see her just after she has emerged from the lock at Avonmouth on 31 March 1973.

(Bernard McCall collection)

Bought by Bennett (UK) Ltd, of Rochester, mainly for work in London docklands, the *Sea Challenge* was collected from Avonmouth on 8 October 1992. The largest tug in the Bennett fleet, she was also chartered to assist container ships using the then-new Thamesport container terminal on the Isle of Grain. By 2003 she had been taken out of service and was converted to a houseboat at Hoo Marina, now known as Port Werburgh, on the River Medway. She was photographed in the funnel colours of her new owner whilst at Avonmouth.

(Danny Lynch)

With Royal Portbury Dock open in the late 1970s and Cory Towage bringing more powerful tugs to the Bristol Channel, C J King had to respond. This response was the *Sea Endeavour* which upon delivery became the most powerful tug in the King fleet. With a 12-cylinder Ruston engine of 3150bhp geared to a single fixed-pitch propeller in a steerable Kort nozzle, she had a bollard pull of 46.5 tonnes. Launched at Richards yard in Great Yarmouth on 1 July 1980, she was delivered to C J King on 31 August. We see her dressed overall in the River Avon on 8 September 1980 after her presentation to the public.

(Cedric Catt)

The **Sea Endeavour** proved to be remarkable in terms of the liveries that she carried. It was not long, of course, before Cory King became simply Cory and we see her below in Cory colours on 5 August 1990. As will be explained later, Cory was taken over by Wijsmuller in 2000 and we see her, upper right, in the colours of that Dutch company in October 2001. Finally Wijsmuller was taken over by Svitzer, a Danish company, and she wears that company's colours in the lower right image at Avonmouth on 17 July 2003.

(Bernard McCall collection; Dominic McCall x 2)

She was sold out of the Svitzer fleet in 2005 following a period laid up in Esbjerg. By 2007 she had been bought by Skånes Entreprenad Service AB, a Swedish company, and had been renamed **Sea Endeavour I** under the flag of Panama. In August 2007, while engaged in towing a barge carrying empty oil tanks from Luleå in northern Sweden, she suffered engine problems and had to go to Umeå for repairs. In July 2008, she was detained in the Danish port of Nakskov and has remained there since then in steadily deteriorating condition.

We now leave the C J King fleet to concentrate on the Cory tugs. The *Falgarth* was driven by a 6-cylinder Deutz engine of 500 bhp geared to a single fixed-pitch propeller. She had a bollard pull of 8.5 tonnes. She was built by P de Vries Lentsch at Alphen a/d Rijn where she was launched on 3 July 1958 and delivered as *Cleddia* on 17 November of that same year. Her owners were the Overseas Towage & Salvage Co Ltd, of London, with Milford Haven Tug Services Ltd as managers. That company had been successful in bidding for a contract to work at Milford Haven and the *Cleddia* was one of two tugs built to service this contract. It was soon evident that these two tugs would be far too small to handle the large tankers which would be using the oil terminals about to open on the Haven and their owners decided to opt out of tug operation. In mid-October 1961, the *Cleddia* was bought by R & J H Rea and renamed *Falgarth* for trading in the Bristol Channel. Also in this photograph, taken at Avonmouth on 13 May 1969, is the *Avongarth*.

(Terry Nelder)

Ownership of the *Falgarth* passed to Cory Ship Towage in 1970. In 1972, she moved to Plymouth after Cory had taken over the towage business of the Reynolds company based there. In early 1980 she was sold to Greek owners and renamed *Aetos*, becoming *Dikefalos Aetos* in 1998 and *Milos* in 2004. At some stage prior to 2011 she was renamed *Kapetan Napoleon* as she was seen off the Greek island of Salamis when named thus in December 2011.

(Danny Lynch)

Between 1969 and 1971 R & J H Rea Ltd took over several smaller towage companies; one of these was James Cooper (Belfast) Ltd which was taken over by Rea in 1969. In 1957, Esso invited tenders for two tugs to handle tankers calling at its new refinery being built at Whitegate near Cobh in the Republic of Ireland. Both tugs were required to have firefighting capability and have a bollard pull in excess of 20 tonnes. The Belfast company won the contract and ordered two tugs from T Mitchison Ltd at Gateshead. Named *Cashel* and *Clonmel*, they immediately proved to be successful. The *Cashel* was launched on 7 November 1958 and completed on 3 April 1959. She was driven by a 6-cylinder British Polar engine of 1364bhp geared to a controllable-pitch propeller. This gave a bollard pull of 22 tonnes. In 1970 ownership was transferred to Cory and three years later, the *Cashel* left Cobh for Avonmouth, being renamed *Portgarth* the following year. In 1981 she was sold to Greek owners and was renamed *Vernicos Martha*, becoming *Aghios Nikolaos* in 1995. She is thought to be still in service. We see her shortly after leaving the lock at Avonmouth on 31 March 1973.

(Bernard McCall collection)

The **Avongarth** was the second of a pair of tugs ordered from the Northwich shipyard of W J Yarwood & Sons in the late 1950s. She was launched on 10 February 1960 and delivered on 2 June. Power came from an 8-cylinder Ruston & Hornsby engine of 870bhp geared to a single fixed-pitch propeller. This gave her a bollard pull of 13.5 tonnes. In 1979 she was transferred to Plymouth. We see her making a rare return to the Bristol Channel as she towed the dredger **Bowqueen** out of Cardiff for breaking up in Spain. Sold out of the Cory fleet in 1989 the **Avongarth** was renamed **Tiverton** but was soon acquired by owners in Portugal and renamed **Galito**. In 1999 she became **San Vicente** (written on the ship as **S Vicente**) with Setubal as her port of registry and was broken up at Lisbon six years later.

(Bernard McCall)

The **Plumgarth** was built at the W J Yarwood & Sons shipyard in Northwich for R & J H Rea. She was launched on 22 October 1959 and delivered on 26 February 1960. Ownership was transferred to Cory in 1970. Power came from an 8-cylinder Ruston & Hornsby engine of 870bhp geared to a single fixed-pitch propeller, giving her a bollard pull of 13.5 tonnes. With the arrival of larger and more powerful tugs in the Bristol Channel after the opening of Royal Portbury Dock, the **Plumgarth** was transferred to Plymouth in 1979. Sold to Greece in 1985, she was renamed **Minotavros** and remains in service.

(Bernard McCall collection)

The **Polgarth** was the first of a pair ordered b R & J H Rea. She went down the slipway at Charles Hill's yard on 25 January 1962 and she was completed on 7 April. Power came from a 6-cylinder Ruston & Hornsby engine of 1080bhp which was geared to a single fixed-pitch propeller. She had a bollard pull of 14.5 tonnes. In 1986 she left the Bristol Channel and was transferred to Foynes but found to be not powerful enough. We see her off Avonmouth on 21 November 1970.

(Bernard McCall collection)

The *Polgarth* awaits her next duty at Avonmouth in May 1983. In late 1987 she returned to Plymouth and was laid up. There seemed to be no future for her and in 1989 she was sold to Sam Evans at Garston for demolition. Before this could begin, indeed before she left Plymouth, she was sold to Divemex Ltd, of Newtown, Powys, for further work and was renamed *Oliver Felix*. Her new owner had a contract for seabed cable trench ploughing.

(Bernard McCall)

As *Oliver Felix* she was chartered to Cory because of delays in bringing other tugs into service and we see her at Avonmouth on 14 January 1990. She passed through the hands of several British owners but the end seemed to have come when she was detained with over 50 defects at Lowestoft on 5 September 2000. Bought by Pounds Marine, she was permitted to sail to Southampton for scrapping. Astonishingly, she escaped yet again and was sold for further trade. She was bought by a Plymouth-based diving company in mid-July 2005 and two years later was renamed *Luvly Jubly*. On 23 October 2007 she suffered a mechanical failure in Weymouth Bay whilst towing a barge from Cowes to Plymouth. The barge drifted aground. Sold for scrapping in late 2011, there was no escape on that occasion.

(Cedric Catt)

The **Pengarth** was the second of the pair of sister tugs built by Charles Hill and followed the **Polgarth**. There is a story that the builder had already started construction of a tug, similar to **Polgarth**, using spare steel within the yard; that tug would ultimately become **Pengarth**. There is no evidence for this story and it seems very unlikely. She was launched on 14 August 1962 and delivered to R & J H Rea on 18 September. We see her in Cory's black & white livery off Avonmouth on 11 July 1970.

(Bernard McCall collection)

The two photographs on this page show the **Pengarth** with a Cory red funnel. Firstly we see her emerging from the lock and into Royal Edward Dock at Avonmouth on 9 July 1988 She and the **Polgarth** had identical propulsion machinery. Her career in the 1990s was disjointed. Sold in March 1991 to a company based in Totnes, she was to have been renamed **Kite** according to some sources but was immediately offered for resale. In August 1991 she was sold to an owner in Grimsby and then in 1996 to a company in Newcastle. This followed an abortive sale to the same company four years previously.

(Bernard McCall)

We see the **Pengarth** off the entrance to Avonmouth. In early 1997 she was sold to Nigerian interests and in April was sold on for use in Togo. Renamed **Vigilant**, she is thought to be still in service and flying the flag of Togo in the ownership of Togo Oil & Marine.

(Danny Lynch)

In the early and mid-1960s numerous changes were taking place within British ports. The British Transport Docks Board had been formed and this had its own tug fleet in some ports. At Cardiff and Barry the towage operations were taken over from BTBD by R & J H Rea Ltd. Clearly, new vessels would be needed. By chance Richards Shipbuilders at Lowestoft had been working on a new design of tug. It was agreed between Rea and Richards that one such vessel would be constructed for evaluation at Cardiff. That vessel was **Lowgarth**. We see her in the company of **Pengarth** and **Sea Challenge** at Avonmouth in August 1983.

(the late Mike Hawkins, Chris Jones collection)

In the event the evaluation period was shorter than intended and orders were placed for four similar but upgraded tugs. The *Lowgarth* was launched on 21 December 1964 and delivered on 28 February 1965. She had a 7-cylinder Ruston & Hornsby engine of 920bhp geared to a fixed-pitch propeller within a steerable Kort nozzle. This gave her a bollard pull of 15 tonnes. She again has the *Sea Challenge* for company as she prepares to lock out at Avonmouth on 7 October 1983. They share the lock with the Norwegian coaster *Hammerstein* outward bound to Antwerp with a cargo of lead.

(Cedric Catt)

The *Lowgarth* worked mainly in South Wales until 1979 when she moved across to the English side of the Bristol Channel and became the preferred tug for assisting vessels in the River Avon or sailing to Sharpness. Here we see her about to swing round the stern of a vessel which is turning to port after entering Royal Edward Dock at Avonmouth on 9 July 1988. The image on page 62 completes the manouvre.

(Bernard McCall)

The **Dalegarth** was the last of four tugs built by Henry Scarr at Hessle for service at the new tanker terminals on Milford Haven. She was launched on 16 February 1960 and completed on 8 June. Power came from a 7-cylinder British Polar engine of 1300bhp geared to a fixed pitch propeller. This gave her a bollard pull of 22 tonnes. The size of oil tankers grew rapidly in the 1960s and the **Dalegarth** and her sisters were outdated by the end of the decade. In 1970, she was sent, along with two of her sister tugs, to service a new Cory contract at the Point Tupper oil refinery in Canada until the arrival of purpose-built tugs. On return, she was based in the Bristol Channel. In 1984, she became the **St Piran** after sale to the Falmouth Towage Company. Sold without change of name in 2007, she was eventually recycled at Ghent in 2012. We see her with **Pengarth** outside the Cory office in the Junction Cut at Avonmouth on 15 June 1979.

(Cedric Catt)

27

The **Butegarth** was one of the four tugs built by Richards at Lowestoft and following on from the evaluation of **Lowgarth** (see pages 24-26). Launched on 26 October 1965, she was completed on 25 January 1966. Her engine was an 8-cylinder Blackstone of 850bhp geared to a single fixed pitch propeller in a steerable Kort nozzle. This combination gave her a bollard pull of 14 tonnes. In 1989 she was sold to Arklow Shipping and renamed **Arklow**; her main role was to assist cement carriers calling at Drogheda to load. In the following year, however, she was sold to owners in Lisbon and renamed **Lutamar**. In mid-2014, she remained in service in Lisbon.

(Bernard McCall collection)

The **Bargarth** was the last of the four tugs from the Richards shipyard in Lowestoft that were based on the design of the **Lowgarth**. As a result of experience learnt from the operation of the previous three, her hull was modified at a very early stage in construction. She was launched on 5 April 1966 and completed on 1 July. In 1986, she was taken to George Prior Engineering Ltd in Lowestoft and there fitted with a retractable bow thruster unit which increased her bollard pull from 14 tonnes to 17 tonnes. In 2002 she was sold to Bilberry Shipping in Waterford without change of name and eight years later came back into British ownership as **Tennaherdhya** when acquired by Keynvor Morlift Ltd in Appledore. Her Kort nozzle is in evidence when seen in drydock at Avonmouth on 14 April 1981.

(Peter Hobday)

In 1971 a consortium of Smit & Cory won a contract to supply tugs at a new oil refinery at Come-By-Chance in Newfoundland, Canada. The two harbour tugs in the contract were **Point James** and **Point Gilbert**. Both tugs were built at the Richard Dunston yard in Hessle and had an English Electric main engine of 2640bhp geared to a controllable-pitch propeller in a steerable Kort nozzle. This gave them a bollard pull of 37 tonnes. The **Point Gilbert** was the first of the pair to be delivered, being launched on 13 April 1972 and completed on 11 September. We see her approaching Avonmouth on 20 July 1980.

(Danny Lynch)

On 28 November 1986 **Point Gilbert** arrived at Lowestoft to be fitted with a retractable Aquamaster bow thruster powered by a separate engine of 671bhp. This modification was made to improve her performance when working stern first as a stern tug. As a further improvement for such work, she was fitted with a towing hook on her foredeck. The bow thruster not only improved manoeuvrability but increased her bollard pull to 45 tonnes. Both tugs were released following the premature closure of the Come-by-Chance refinery. The success of **Point James** in Royal Portbury Dock (see pages 32-33) soon resulted in **Point Gilbert** also being brought back. Sold in mid-2007, she was briefly renamed **Point Gilbert I** before being taken over by Russian owners and renamed **Gangut**. She was photographed passing Battery Point in April 1997.

(Bernard McCall)

The Eastern Arm in Avonmouth's Royal Edward Dock was unusually devoid of shipping on 1 May 1983 with the exception of a coaster at West Wharf 5 in the distance. *Point James* and *Point Gilbert* lie at O Berth. The *Point James* was launched at Hessle on 13 June 1972 and delivered on 7 November. The oil crisis in the Middle East in the early 1970s resulted in the premature closure of the Come-By-Chance refinery with the tugs becoming redundant. The *Point James* was brought back from Canada mainly to provide towage at the new Royal Portbury Dock opened in August 1977.

(Bernard McCall)

About seven weeks after the photograph above was taken, the *Point James* is seen awaiting a vessel outside Royal Portbury Dock where she was proving to be so successful. The precise date was 19 June 1983. After the arrival of *Portgarth* (see page 46), *Point James* was deployed to Belfast where she arrived on 8 July 1985. On 23 January 1996 when returning from Belfast to Londonderry *Point James* suffered a fuel supply problem and the crew had to abandon ship. They were rescued by helicopter and the tug was rescued the following day by another Cory vessel.

(Bernard McCall)

Photographs of **Point James** with a Cory red funnel are surprisingly rare. We see her approaching Royal Portbury lock on 6 August 1992. In mid-May 1999 she was sold to owners in the Dominican Republic with delivery being deferred until early 2000. The sale was not completed and the tug was repossessed. In 2002 she was renamed **Saint James** but retained her British registry. She was understood to have been sold to Turkish owners in 2005 and then hoisted the flag of Panama. Her subsequent work pattern is unclear as she was noted at Vigo in 2007 and Las Palmas in 2008. At the time, her funnel and upperworks colours differed from those noted in 2006 so she may have been sold yet again. It is certain, though, that she arrived at Aliaga for recycling on 18 April 2009.

(Danny Lynch)

The **Edengarth** began life as one four tugs built to work at Milford Haven. She was launched at the Great Yarmouth yard of Richards (Shipbuilders) Ltd on 29 April 1976 and completed as **Edengarth** for the Rea Towing Company Ltd on 19 July. Her engine was a 16-cylinder Ruston of 3520bhp and was geared to a controllable-pitch propeller in a steerable Kort nozzle. She moved to Avonmouth in 1997 and we see her there on 27 February in that year.

(Peter Hobday)

In the late 1990s an oil terminal at Whiddy Island in southern Ireland reopened and the towage contract was allocated to Smit International. However, because tanker visits would be infrequent it was agreed that tugs would be chartered from Cory when needed. The first tug to be thus used was the **Edengarth** in April 1998. She was sold in the following year and, now registered at Kingstown, left the Bristol Channel as **Eden** on 5 September 1999 as seen in this photograph. By the end of the year, she had been renamed **Oriental Tug No. 2**. Later changes of name saw her become **Sumerian 2** (2003), **Mitra O** (2006), and **Prawira Dua** (2007). Under that name she currently flies the flag of Indonesia.

(Bernard McCall)

The **Bargarth** has the distinction of being the final ship to have been built by Scott & Sons at Bowling on the northen bank of the River Clyde. Her history is interesting. She was launched at the Bowling shipyard on 25 June 1979 and on 12 November was delivered as **Laggan** to Forth Tugs Ltd. This company had been renamed from Grangemouth and Forth Towing Company in February 1977 in order to mark its work at the Hound Point terminal on the Firth of Forth from which crude oil was to be exported. In fact the Clyde Shipping Company and Cory Ship Towage had jointly taken over the company in 1972. The order for the **Laggan** was part of a 4-ship order, the other tugs being the **Carron** which was a sistership and the **Hallgarth** and **Holmgarth** which were intended for the Cory fleet in South Wales as we shall soon see. With tanker traffic increasing at Grangemouth, the design of the two Forth tugs differed from that of the other pair because they had to be fitted with firefighting equipment. To increase their height, an extra deck was fitted below the bridge deck and the layout of the engine room was modified to permit the fitting of pumping equipment. The **Laggan** had two 6-cylinder Ruston engines, each of 1100bhp and geared to Voith-Schneider propellers. This combination gave her a bollard pull of 24 tonnes. In 1987 she was renamed **Forth** when the previous holder of this name was sold. Having been acquired by Wijsmuller and then Svitzer, she left the latter's fleet in 2003 when purchased by operators in Waterford by whom she was renamed **Fastnet Nore**. She passes Battery Point on 23 April 2004.

(Bernard McCall)

The **Holmgarth**, photographed off Battery Point in May 2001, and sister tug **Hallgarth** represented a new thinking at Cory Towage. For various reasons, British tug operators had been reluctant to introduce multi-directional propulsion systems although these were popular in other parts of the world. In 1978, Cory Towage decided to place an order for four tugs fitted with German Voith-Schneider directional propellers. Two of these were to be firefighting tugs for work on the Firth of Forth as we have just noted but the other two were destined for South Wales. This four-tug order was the last received by the long-established building yard of Scott & Sons, at Bowling on the River Clyde. Having been launched on 18 December 1978, the **Holmgarth** was the first of the Welsh pair to be completed, delivery being made on 2 May 1979. In autumn 1992 she transferred to the River Mersey where she had the distinction of being the first Voith Schneider tractor tug to be employed on the river. She returned to the Bristol Channel in 1998 and remained there, apart from a brief stint in Dublin during summer 1999, until her sale. Having given excellent service for almost thirty years, she was sold to Fowey Harbour Commissioners in 2008 and renamed **Morgawr**. The livery, seen here for the first time in this book, will be explained on the following pages.

(Bernard McCall)

Any tugs that were in service between 2000 and 2002 had three very different liveries. In 2000 Cory Towage was taken over by Wijsmuller, a huge Dutch towage and salvage company and it was not long before the tug fleet began to be repainted with the prominent vivid blue that we have seen on the *Holmgarth* on the previous page. In the following year, however, Wijsmuller itself was taken over by Svitzer, a long-established Danish towage company that had become part of the huge Mærsk-Möller group. The blue paint was scarcely dry before the tugs were again repainted, now into Svitzer colours.

Before those changes we see the *Hallgarth* in Cory colours off Battery Point in March 2000 with the Chinese bulk carrier *Tai Gu Hai* making her approach in the background.

(Dominic McCall)

The *Hallgarth* was photographed in Svitzer livery off Royal Portbury Dock on 23 April 2004 having assisted an outward bound vessel and awaiting an inward one. Both are just visible in the distance, Launched on 15 February 1979 and delivered on 28 June, the *Hallgarth* eventually followed sister tug *Holmgarth* to Cornwall, being acquired by the A&P Group in Falmouth by whom she was renamed *St Piran* also in 2008. Both tugs are driven by two 6-cylinder Ruston engines with a total output of 2190bhp and geared to two Voith-Schneider propellers. This gives them a bollard pull of 23.5 tonnes.

(Dominic McCall)

Cory Ship Towage had been pleased with the performance of some Japanese tugs chartered in the mid-1980s and looked to Japan once again in 1990 when seeking new tonnage. The choice was the *Iwashima Maru*. Cory already had good contacts with J P Knight, a Medway-based towage company which had also just bought a tug in Japan and it was agreed that this tug would be delivered to the UK along with the *Iwashima Maru* by a heavy-lift ship named *Project Arabia*. Delays were encountered for various reasons and it was not until 8 February 1991 that the *Project Arabia* arrived at Southampton. After unloading the *Iwashima Maru* was towed to Avonmouth by *Point Gilbert*, arriving on 13 February. She was then taken to Sharpness for refit and was renamed *Avongarth*. We see her in the City Docks when she was presented to the public.

(Danny Lynch)

The *Iwashima Maru* had been launched at the Kobe shipyard of Kanagawa Zosen K K on 19 April 1980 and delivered to her Japanese owners on 17 June. She is driven by two 6-cylinder Niigata engines, each of 1300bhp and geared to two Z-peller propulsion units. This gives her a bollard pull of 35 tonnes. We see her as *Avongarth* heading down channel at speed on 12 August 2007.

(Kevin Jones)

In the early 1980s, Cory Towage was seeking to expand and won a contract to provide towage services at Chevron's Malongo oil terminal in Angola. Two tugs were built at the McTay yard at Bromborough and the first was named **Eldergarth**. Launched on 3 July 1981 and delivered on 1 October, she was initially registered at Westport, County Mayo. She and sister tug **Rowangarth** left the Mersey for Angola in late November 1982. In May 1999 the **Eldergarth** was sold to Shannon Tugs Ltd and renamed **Shannon**. Power comes from two 8-cylinder Niigata engines each of 1600bhp and geared to twin stern-mounted Z-peller propulsion units giving her a bollard pull of 42 tonnes. This method of propulsion is known as azimuthing stern drive (ASD) and the tug has the distinction of being the first British-built tug thus driven.

We see her in three different liveries. Upper right, painting into Wijsmuller livery has just begun whilst careful observation of the lower right photograph will reveal that the Maltese Cross of Svitzer has been added to her funnel. The yellow diamond on her funnel in the image below would have previously contained the letters S.T.L., these being the initials of Shannon Tugs Ltd. The photograph was taken at Avonmouth on 12 February 2001.

(Peter Hobday, Bernard McCall x 2)

The **Westgarth** and **Thorngarth** were both built at the Yokosaka shipyard of Hanazaki Zosensho K K. The **Westgarth** was the first of the pair to be launched, this taking place on 11 April 1983. She was delivered to Tokyo-based Daito Unyu K K as **Yashima** on 9 May. She was acquired by Cory Towage Ltd in July 1992 with delivery deferred until October. Power comes from two 6-cylinder Niigata main engines, each of 1300bhp and geared to two Z-peller multidirectional propellers. This gives her a bollard pull of 40 tonnes. She arrived at Avonmouth in January 1993 and has rarely left the area other than to work in South and West Wales.

She was delivered directly from Japan and we see her, right, arriving for the first time on a sunny day in January 1993.

(Danny Lynch)

Below, she passes Battery Point seven months later, now in full Cory livery.

(Bernard McCall)

Below right, she was in Wijsmuller livery when assisting a bulk carrier towards Royal Portbury Dock in May 2001.

(Bernard McCall)

In early 1991, Cory Towage won the 5-yearly contract to provide towage services at Milford Haven. The oil companies on the Haven at that time were demanding improved specifications for the tug fleet and Cory Towage was compelled to look to Japan for suitable tugs. The **Thorngarth** was launched at the Yokosuka yard of Hanasaki Zosensho K K in Japan on 8 August 1983 and completed on 6 September. Like the **Westgarth**, she was delivered to Daito Unyu K K and was originally named **Tenzan**. She is also powered by two 6-cylinder Niigata engines geared to two Z-peller propulsion units but with an individual output of 1699bhp these engines are more powerful than those of the **Westgarth**

and they provide a bollard pull of 45 tonnes. Although bought in July 1991, she was not handed over until December. Then renamed **Thorngarth**, she left Yokohama on 8 January 1992 and sailed under her own power to Avonmouth. Following drydocking and refurbishment, she entered service at Milford Haven in April 1992. After leaving the Haven, she moved to the Mersey and then arrived in the Bristol Channel in 2010, her first duty at Avonmouth being on 20 October 2010. We see her alongside the tanker **Maersk Christiansbro** on 23 July 2011.

(Bernard McCall)

41

The **HT Scimitar** was the first of the pair of tugs built at the McTay yard for the Dover Harbour Board. She was launched on 17 April 1984 and delivered as **Deft** on 8 June. Propulsion details are identical to those of the **HT Cutlass** seen below. Transfer to the Thames fleet of Howard Smith saw her renamed **Shorne** prior to being taken over by Adsteam. In August 2006, Adsteam decided to increase towage competition on the Humber by introducing its own cut-rate operation to which it gave the name Humber Tugs Ltd. Eventually a fleet of five tugs was established, all transferred from other areas and the **Shorne** became **HT Scimitar**. However also in 2006 negotiations started for Svitzer to take over Adsteam and this was completed in 2007. In early 2009, the tug was transferred from the Humber to South Wales. Both tugs left for Puerto Cabello in the same circumstances as we see on page 63.

(Bernard McCall)

The **HT Cutlass**, arriving at Avonmouth on 27 January 2012, was the second of the pair from the McTay yard being launched for the Dover Harbour Board as **Dextrous** on 15 May 1984 and delivered during July. The fendering system of the tugs, especially at the stern, was designed to assist in the berthing of large cross-channel ferries. Power comes from two 6-cylinder Ruston engines, each of 1337bhp and geared to two Voith-Schneider propellers. This gives the tugs a bollard pull of 29 tonnes. She became **Cobham** in 2000 after being acquired by Howard Smith Towage for work on the River Thames but ownership was transferred to Adsteam in the following year. Some three years later, she was transferred to the Humber Tugs fleet. It was in spring 2007 that Svitzer took over Adsteam and she became **HT Cutlass**. Both tugs were transferred to South Wales with occasional visits to the English side of the Bristol Channel. Not powerful enough for much of the work required, both were eventually sold in 2013 to Zulia Towing & Barge Co, of Maracaibo, and they left Avonmouth on 17 July 2013.

(Chris Jones)

The **Svitzer Bevois**, photographed passing Battery Point on 28 May 2012, was launched by McTay Marine on 2 June 1985 and delivered as **Sir Bevois** on 22 August to the Southampton, Isle of Wight and South of England Royal Mail Steam Packet plc, better known as Red Funnel, in late August 1995. The Red Funnel Group had been acquired by Associated British Ports six years earlier and the Group was sold in 2001. Red Funnel Towage was formed that same year but was sold in 2002 to Adsteam Marine Ltd. Named after the legendary founder of Southampton, she was one of a pair of tugs ordered by Red Funnel to work in the Solent and was the third vessel to carry this name. Power comes from two 6-cylinder Kromhout engines, each of 1360bhp, driving two Schottel directional propellers. This gives her a bollard pull of 34 tonnes. Adsteam was itself taken over by Svitzer. In 2008, she transferred to the Bristol Channel, at first working in South Wales but then moving to the English side and based in Bristol. She was sold to Swedish owners in December 2014 and renamed **Beaver**.

(Bernard McCall)

The *Stackgarth* was one of a group of tugs built at the Hessle shipyard of Richard Dunston in the late 1980s and early 1990s for the Tees Towing Company. She was launched as *Eston Cross* on 20 February 1985 and completed on 29 March. Power comes from two 6-cylinder Ruston engines totalling 3400bhp and geared to twin Aquamaster multidirectional propellers mounted forward. She has a bollard pull of 43 tonnes. In August 1990, Tees Towing was taken over by Cory Towage but the *Eston Cross* was not renamed until she transferred to Milford Haven in 1994 and assumed the local name of *Stackgarth*. After arrival in the local Bristol Channel fleet, she was generally used as bow tug because of her forward drive, general layout and power. In this view, a heaving line has just been thrown to the tug from the bow of the tanker *Euro Song* inward bound with aviation fuel on 19 October 2003.

(Bernard McCall)

In mid-January 1997 the **Stackgarth** transferred to Liverpool and then moved to Belfast in May but returned to the Mersey in September of that same year. She transferred to Swansea in October 1998. In the previous month Howard Smith Towage, which operated the tug fleet in the Welsh port, announced that it would cease service at Swansea from 9 October because of reduced demand and Cory took over towage responsibilities. The **Stackgarth** was the first Cory tug to be based in Swansea after the departure of Howard Smith Towage. In summer 1999, her superstructure was modified to improve visibility. She soon became part of the Bristol-based fleet. She later moved to the River Tyne and in 2010 was sold to an operator in Waterford by whom she was renamed **Fastnet Nore**. In 2013, she was bareboat chartered by Stadt Sjøtransport AS, based in the Norwegian port of Florø, and was repainted into the colours of this company.

The arrival of the **Stackgarth** in the local fleet in 1999 ensured that she was just in time to see the varied livery changes of the next two years. On the right we see her with a Cory red funnel that was to be shortlived. She was assisting the bulk carrier **Tetien** on 25 June 1999. Below right, she is in Wijsmuller livery along with **Point Gilbert** on 15 August 2000. Finally, below, we see her in Svitzer livery at the bow of the bulk carrier **Sea Daisy** on 7 April 2003.

(Bernard McCall, Peter Hobday x 2)

For over twenty years the Damen company based in the Netherlands has had hulls built in other yards and then kept them in reserve until ordered by a customer. One such example was the **Portgarth**. The hull of this tug was built at the SevMash shipyard in Severodvinsk and launched on 3 November 1993. It was then towed to the Damen yard at Gorinchem to await a buyer. This proved to be Cory Towage Ltd and the tug was completed on 30 March 1995. An example of the ASD Tug 3110 design, the **Portgarth** has the distinction of being the first standard shiphandling tug delivered to a British company by Damen.

(Bernard McCall)

The **Portgarth** is driven by two 9-cylinder Kromhout engines with a total power of 3980bhp and these are geared to two stern-mounted Z-peller units. She has a bollard pull of 50 tonnes. It was always intended that she would be based at Avonmouth and Royal Portbury Dock but she has spent periods in other ports such as Milford Haven. There seemed to be some confusion about the correct livery when this photograph was taken in July 2002. Only the lower part of her funnel remains in Wijsmuller blue; her hull has been painted Svitzer black - but rather surprisingly the Wijsmuller name has been added.

(Bernard McCall)

Owned by Trieste-based Tripmare, the **Uran** arrived in the Bristol Channel on 10 April 2003 for a short-term charter to Svitzer. She replaced the **Shannon** (see pages 38/39) which had moved from the Bristol Channel to the Mersey when the **Svitzer Bristol** and **Svitzer Brunel** had not yet been delivered. She was launched by Astilleros Armon at Navia in Spain on 26 May 1988 and delivered to Tripmare on 20 October. She is driven by two MaK 9-cylinder engines, each of 2039bhp driving two stern-mounted directional propellers. She has a bollard pull of 50 tonnes. Although not repainted in Svitzer colours, she was renamed **Danegarth** and reverted to **Uran** on completion of the charter, leaving the Bristol Channel on 20 November 2003. In 2011 she was sold to Cuxhaven-based **Otto Wulf** and was renamed **Wulf 7** after arrival at her new home port in early November.

(Dominic McCall)

The *Svitzer Moira* is a sistership of the *Svitzer Ellerby* below. Launched on 19 November 1997, she was delivered to the Hong Kong Salvage & Towage Co Ltd as *Peng Chau* on 9 January 1998, just one month before her sister. Her purchase by Howard Smith, however, came a year later as it was in September 1999 that she was acquired and her name was amended to *Peng* for the delivery voyage. In November 1999 she was renamed *Lady Moira* for work on the Humber with Grimsby as her port of registry. She was taken over by Adsteam in 2001 and then by Svitzer in April 2007. She was renamed *Svitzer Moira* on 11 August 2007. She started work in the Bristol Channel on the morning of 3 July 2011 when she was stern tug on one of the Grimaldi vehicle carriers. She was photographed on 15 May 2012. Careful observation of these recent photographs will reveal a change in the funnel logo on Svitzer tugs. It was in 2007 that the company's traditional Maltese Cross was replaced by a propeller.

(Bernard McCall)

The *Svitzer Ellerby*, photographed on 18 May 2014, was built by Imamura Zosen at Kure in Japan. She was launched on 12 December 1997 and delivered to Hong Kong Salvage & Towage Co Ltd on 9 February 1998. Power comes from two 6-cylinder Niigata engines with a total output of 3602bhp and geared to two Z-peller propulsion units. She has a bollard pull of 47 tonnes. Her work in the Far East was shortlived as she was acquired by Howard Smith during the summer of 1998. Initially renamed *Lady Emma,* that was soon modified to *Lady Emma H* and she worked on the River Medway. Once Adsteam had taken over Howard Smith she was transferred to the Humber and renamed *Adsteam Ellerby* in 2005 and then *Svitzer Ellerby* in 2007. In late summer 2011, she arrived in the Bristol Channel to take over from *Svitzer Brunel*, her first duty in the area being on the afternoon tide of 24 September.

(Kevin Jones)

The Svitzer takeover of Wijsmuller was bound to lead to significant changes in towage fleets not only in the Bristol Channel but throughout the UK as Svitzer would henceforth have a presence in most of the major British ports. This would mean that tugs could easily be transferred from one port to another according to commercial and operational needs. Most of the smaller companies now subsumed within the Svitzer fleet named their tugs according to local traditions. At first Svitzer attempted to continue this policy and thus we received two new tugs named *Svitzer Bristol* and *Svitzer Brunel*. The aim was laudable but soon became meaningless in practice as tugs were moved to areas where the name had no local significance.

When Svitzer took over the Wijsmuller fleet, an early decision was to have two new tugs built for the Bristol area. The order was given to Astilleros Zamakona whose yard is at Vizcaya on the outskirts of Bilbao. The first of the pair to be delivered was the *Svitzer Bristol* which arrived on 15 July 2003. She had been launched as *Bristolgarth* on 16 April. In 2011 she moved to the Solent and then to the Humber in 2014.

(Bernard McCall)

In fact the two local tugs were followed by two similar tugs named *Svitzer Bidston* and *Svitzer Bootle* destined, not surprisingly, for the River Mersey. The tugs are powered by two 6-cylinder Niigata main engines with a total output of 4400bhp and geared to two Z-peller propulsion units. This gives them a bollard pull of 59 tonnes. Although noted briefly on the Clyde and Solent in 2010, the *Svitzer Brunel* has been based on the River Thames since 2012. She was launched as *Severngarth* on 15 June 2003 and delivered to Svitzer on 16 September. We see her on 13 July 2010 assisting the *Orange Star* which was a regular caller with fruit juice from South America. The *Orange Star* had been converted from the Blue Star refrigerated cargo ship *Andalucia Star*.

(Chris Jones)

The arrival of the brand new *Svitzer Sky* on 12 February 2009 was unexpected. She is an example of the Damen ASD2411 standard design. This design has become extremely popular with tug operators throughout the world. The tugs were designed for two-man operation although in the Bristol Channel and elsewhere in the UK they have a crew of three. The hull of the tug was built at the Song Cam shipyard in Haiphong, Vietnam, with completion at the Damen shipyard in Gorinchem. We see her at speed in the Bristol Channel on 19 April 2009.

(Kevin Jones)

In the winter of 2013/14, the **Triton** was chartered from Iskes Towage and Salvage, a company based at IJmuiden in the Netherlands. This tug was built by Dearsan Gemi at Tuzla in Turkey and delivered in May 2008. Power comes from two 12-cylinder engines, each of 2600bhp and manufactured by the Anglo Belgian Corporation at Ghent. These engines are geared to two Schottel directional propulsion units and the tug has a bollard pull of 70 tonnes.

(Kevin Jones)

In our final pages we shall look at tugs in various settings around the area. We begin with a historic view of the **Pengarth** berthed by the Charles Hill shipyard on 11 January 1977. This industrial landscape has been virtually obliterated and it is now difficult to imagine that it was such a hive of activity.

(Cedric Catt)

On the back cover, we see the **Avongarth** in the River Avon. The reason for her presence was that she was escorting the passenger vessel **Balmoral** which is about to pass beneath the M5 motorway bridge on 8 April 2006. It had become a requirement that **Balmoral** and similar large vessels should have an escort for transits of the river and we shall see three more examples in Volume 2. As this book is being compiled in early 2015, there is optimism that **Balmoral** will return to cruising in the Bristol Channel in the near future.

(Dominic McCall)

A fine close-up of the *Westgarth* assisting a bulk carrier into Royal Portbury Dock on 31 May 2007. Despite the fact that they look very similar and the fact that they have consecutive yard numbers from the same builder, the *Westgarth* and *Thorngarth* are not sister ships. The *Westgarth* was the first of the pair to be launched.

(Kevin Jones)

This interesting view enables the reader to identify some of the differences between the Japanese-built tugs *Westgarth*, with a line already attached to the stern of the inward bound vehicle carrier *Atlantic Breeze*, and *Avongarth*, nearer the camera and hurrying to take up position on the starboard quarter of the same vessel. The date was 22 July 2000 and the *Avongarth* was already in Wijsmuller livery but only the mast of the *Westgarth* had been painted by that date. The reader should find several other detail differences.

(Dominic McCall)

On page 49, we noted that the **Svitzer Bristol** and **Svitzer Brunel** had been designed and built to work at our local port. Here is the **Svitzer Bristol** doing exactly that work on 23 April 2004, namely holding the bulk carrier **Apj Jit** in position at the entrance to Royal Portbury Dock as the force of the incoming tide seeks to push the vessel away from the breakwater.

(Dominic McCall)

This splendid view, taken from the stern of the **CSAV Rio Puelo** inward bound on 18 January 2009 and entering the lock at Avonmouth, clearly shows both the considerable beam of the **Svitzer Sky** along with her angled funnels and exhaust uptakes. She was delivered from her builders in Vietnam in October 2008 but spent some time in the Netherlands for trials and commissioning before coming to the Bristol Channel. Driven by two 16-cylinder Caterpillar engines totalling 5710bhp and geared to two directional propellers, she has a bollard pull of 70 tonnes. She remained in the local fleet for only a year before being transferred to Felixstowe.

(Chris Jones)

The **Georgios C**, having discharged grain from the Great Lakes, is assisted into the lock at Avonmouth by C J King's **Sea Challenge** on a sunny 15 May 1978. There is not a high-visibility jacket in sight - how things change! In the background to the left is a cargo vessel sporting the controversial P&O livery.

(Cedric Catt)

A vivid reminder of how bad conditions can be in the Bristol Channel even just off the breakwaters. On 8 December 1990 the **Sea Challenge** had to live up to her name as she and the **Point Gilbert** at the stern struggled to bring the Iranian cargo ship **Iran Abad** around the north breakwater in readiness to approach the lock. The fact that the cargo ship was in light condition and therefore high out of the water made the situation even more difficult.

(Peter Hobday)

The photographer was astonishingly fortunate to find the **Stackgarth** in a solitary shaft of sunlight as she heads out towards the Welsh Hook buoy where she will meet an incoming bulk carrier. No doubt the residents of the caravans in the background at Redcliffe Bay would have welcomed some of that sunlight.

(Dominic McCall)

Initially using tugs to handle fishing vessels at IJmuiden, Iskes Towage & Salvage Ltd, the company owning the *Triton* (see page 51), has expanded rapidly in recent years and now handles the largest vessels using the North Sea Canal to visit Amsterdam in addition to salvage, offshore work and windfarm support. During her charter to Svitzer, she was used in ports on both sides of the Bristol Channel. We see her passing Battery Point on 8 January 2014 assisting the bulk carrier *City of Dubrovnik*.

(Bernard McCall)

In the late 1980s, Danish roll-on/roll-off vessels were used on a relatively short-lived service importing fruit and vegetables on trailers from Bulgaria, usually from Bourgas with a call at Limassol in Cyprus.

On 9 July 1988 the **Lowgarth** assists the **Mercandian Ocean** to swing after leaving the lock at Avonmouth.

(Bernard McCall)

On page 42 we reported the sale of the *HT Cutlass* and *HT Scimitar* to operators in Venezuela. The pair of them were delivered by the heavy lift ship *HHL Venice* photographed on 17 July 2013 just after leaving the lock with *Svitzer Moira* in attendance. The *Svitzer Anglia* was being delivered from the River Tees at the same time.

(Chris Jones)

Battery Point at Portishead is one of very few places in the UK where it is possible to see as many as six or even seven tugs assisting a large vessel. With a draught of over 14 metres and a length of 240 metres, the bulk carrier **GL Qushan** is one of the largest callers in recent years bringing coal from Puerto Drummond in Colombia. She was attended by six tugs as she arrived on 19 September 2012. Readers should note that the bow tug, ***Svitzer Moira***, is secured bow-to-bow to the bulk carrier and is therefore going astern as she tows the ship.

(Bernard McCall)